FINI
HEART

FOUNDATIONS OF LIFE
BUILDING DREAMS
TRANSFORMING LIVES

ANNABELLA NASSETTI

WM

Find Your Heart

Annabella Nassetti

First published in May 2025

W&M Publishing

ISBN 978-1-917265-48-5 Pbk

A CIP catalogue record for this book is available from the British Library.

CONTENTS

DEDICATION

This book is dedicated to Assia and Monica,
and the part they continue to play in my life.

This is my way of keeping them alive,
and I know they would be proud of what I am doing.

I am bringing the intangible into the tangible,
guided by the strength of my spirit—
one that has never doubted its direction.

Thank you, Mum, for your guidance.

Thank you, Rosemary, for your unwavering support.

THANK YOU

PERSONAL MENTORS & INSPIRATIONS

Rosemary Warcup and Marisa Peer

"Marisa Peer's work was a turning point in my life. After years of searching for deeper healing, I discovered Rapid Transformational Therapy (RTT), and it instantly shifted something within me. Unlike other approaches I had tried, RTT cut straight to the core, allowing me to finally release the patterns that had held me back for so long.

Meeting Marisa in person was a profoundly moving experience — thanking her for the impact she had on my life was one of those full-circle moments that reaffirmed everything I was working toward.

She not only introduced me to a method that transformed my life, but also inspired me to become a therapist myself.

FAMILY & LOVED ONES

The ones who have shaped my heart and journey.

To Assia and Monica, whose memory fuels my strength and purpose... *every* day.

To my mother, for her unwavering presence in my heart.

PROFESSIONAL & CREATIVE INFLUENCES

Those who helped bring this book to life.

To Dr. Harbeen Arora, for believing in my vision and giving me the platform to amplify my voice.

SPECIAL MENTION

The people who have stood by me unconditionally.

To Manuela and Ettore, my sister and brother, for always being close.

To my father, for the creative business inspiration you are and for not prioritising me.

To Flavia, who was a foundational part of my journey and played an important role in my growth.

To Carly, my love and my safe place.

Thank you for your unwavering support, your kindness, and for bringing light into my life with love, warmth, understanding, and laughter.

AND, OF COURSE

To my friends and family who have stood by me through every challenge, reminding me of my strength and purpose—this book is for you.

WELCOME

WELCOME

My journey began in product design, where I was fascinated by the beauty of objects and their ability to transform everyday life. It was never just about aesthetics — it was about functionality, purpose, and the way objects interact with space to enhance our experience.

From there, I expanded into interior architecture and construction, applying the same principles of balance, flow, and efficiency on a larger scale.

Designing a space is not just about making it look good; it's about creating an environment that supports the way we live, think, and feel.

I became known for my ability to see potential where others saw limitations, reshaping homes to maximize space, light, and energy. But over time, I realized something deeper—I wasn't just designing homes; I was shaping the lives of the people who lived in them.

This understanding became even more personal when I was forced to redesign my own life.

After surviving a life-altering accident, I spent 25 years in coping mode, pushing forward without truly feeling.

When I finally allowed myself to heal, I discovered that the same principles I had applied to design—foundations, structure, and flow—were also the key to personal transformation.

That's what led me to coaching and RTT therapy.

Just like a home needs a solid foundation, our minds and bodies need alignment, clarity, and intentionality to thrive.

Today, my work bridges both worlds:

I design spaces that nurture the soul, and I guide people to rebuild their inner world, just as I once rebuilt my own.

This book is for anyone who feels stuck, disconnected, or in search of clarity. Whether you are an entrepreneur, a creative, a leader, or someone navigating life's transitions, my hope is that my story will help you see obstacles as opportunities for reinvention, find balance between ambition and well-being, and understand how both your environment and your mindset shape your success.

This is how I transformed my career, my mindset, and my purpose.

And how, by mastering the art of design—both in spaces and in self—you too can create a life that is truly worth living.

BEGINNINGS

1 FOUNDATIONS OF LIFE

'The most important words you say in your life are thewords you say to yourself'

MARISA PEER

Let me start by saying this: *life is messy.*

It doesn't come with instructions, and when it does, the pages are often missing.

For me, life started in Milan, the design capital of the world, where I grew up breathing beauty and function. Milan isn't just about fashion runways and tailored suits—though they're hard to ignore—it's about product design, cars, boats, furniture, and the kind of innovation that shapes how we live.

I was surrounded by this energy and, indirectly, by the rhythms of high fashion, a world that effortlessly marries aesthetics with purpose.

But beauty isn't just what you see—it's what you create.

My mother, Tita, embodied this philosophy.

My mother, Tita, captured before she became ill – a source of endless love, strength, inspiration in my life.

She designed our home to be both functional and beautiful, where every detail served a purpose. It wasn't just a house; it was a blueprint for living. A garden as big as a football pitch, a swimming pool, baby cycling lanes - everything was designed to encourage movement, growth, and connection.

It gave me the structure I needed to thrive.

But life isn't always so well-designed.

When I was seven, my mother passed away after a long battle with cancer. Her loss left a void I couldn't understand.

There was no manual for how to process grief at that age, so I didn't - I moved.

Left: Nonna Gea's impeccable style and grace became an enduring inspiration, shaping my view of beauty, balance, and timeless design.

My passion for diving started very young at home.

I kicked footballs, jumped, swam, and cycled my way through the void. I was always running, always keeping myself busy with activities in the garden, searching—or, in hindsight, searching for something I couldn't quite name.

Looking back, I realize that even in the cracks, there is meaning. Life, like design, isn't about *perfection* - it's about *adaptation.*

It's about taking what's broken and using it to build something stronger. My early years taught me that beauty isn't just in the finished product; it's in the process, in the effort it takes to build.

Fast forward to today, and these lessons are at the heart of everything I do. As a designer and building contractor, I'm committed to creating homes—spaces where people live, dream, and grow. It's not just about making something beautiful; it's about balance. It's about honouring the foundations that shape us, both in our homes and in our lives.

This book reflects my journey. It's about the cracks that didn't break me, the foundations I rebuilt, and the resilience that came from finding purpose in chaos.

I hope that in these pages, you'll find inspiration to embrace your own cracks, lay your own foundations, and design a life that's unapologetically yours.

How you do it and what tools you use to get there—*that's what this book is all about.*

2 EARLY INSPIRATIONS

'Only from the heart you can touch the sky.'

RUMI

Milan wasn't just my hometown; it was a living, breathing museum of design. *Everywhere* I turned, there was something extraordinary—sleek cars, glossy wooden boats that glided through lake waters like art, furniture that balanced function and beauty, and of course, the unmistakable hum of high fashion.

Growing up in this city wasn't just about seeing beauty—it was about *understanding* how beauty shaped the world.

I grew up in a house where design wasn't an afterthought; it was the backbone of how we lived.

My mother, Tita, had an innate sense of how to make things work together seamlessly.

Our home was a masterpiece of Milanese design.

It was multifunctional, aesthetically driven, and perfectly balanced. Every piece of furniture, every corner of the house, was thought out and designed with precision.

My childhood home was designed to be functional and beautiful.

It wasn't just a space to live in—it was a sanctuary that taught me how to value form and function in perfect harmony.

From an early age, I was obsessed with pens. Not just any pens—Bic pens, the most ordinary, everyday kind. I had to have them.

The weight of them in my hand, the way the ink glided onto the page, the smoothness of a perfect stroke—it fascinated me. Hand drawing became something I was drawn to that became what grounded me through a distracting life.

At the time, I didn't fully understand why I was so captivated by it. But looking back, I realize now—it wasn't just about the pens. It wasn't just about the handwriting. It was about identity. About structure.

About finding something to hold onto.

Maybe it was my way of creating a sense of order in a world that felt *unpredictable.*

While my home provided structure, I was the opposite: unacademic, unfocused, and always keeping myself entertained with some form of sport.

My mother nicknamed me *Flea.*

The only class I was effortlessly good at was art.

From the very first day of kindergarten, I refused to fit in. While the other kids sat quietly around miniature tables, their heads resting on their arms for nap time, I couldn't get it. Instead, I fled—running straight out of the classroom to go home.

My mother's surprise at seeing me back home so soon earned me a nickname that stuck: *Flea*.

I was always escaping, always in motion, always seeking.

Sports became my greatest outlet. Football (a daily routine with my brother Ettore), volleyball, swimming, cycling, basketball, and skiing, my favourite—if it involved movement, I was in.

My energy was endless, and my father, who often returned from business trips with my favourite grape-flavoured Bubble Yum, encouraged my passion.

Those moments, small as they were, formed some of my most cherished childhood memories.

But my childhood wasn't all harmony.

Skiing has always been my passion. How the mindset sets the style.
From enjoying to racing depending on the mood.

Water-skiing a less favourite - on the Italian Ligurian coast.

Christmas and birthday parties and torment.

As the youngest of three, I often found myself at the mercy of my older siblings.

One particularly memorable Christmas gift—a microscope—became the centrepiece of their experiment to see a teardrop up close. To achieve their goal, they made it their mission to reduce me to tears. I cried, of course, but not just from their teasing. I cried because even as a child, I felt acutely aware of the gaps in my life, the moments of loneliness that no microscope could ever capture.

Still, those years shaped me in ways I didn't fully understand at the time.

Being surrounded by advanced technology, impeccable design, and the best of Milanese craftsmanship left an imprint on me. I began to see the world differently, noticing not just how things looked, but how they worked. I became fascinated by beautiful things—not for their aesthetics alone, but for the way they functioned, the purpose they served.

Looking back, I realize my childhood wasn't just a time of play—it was my first real education in design.

It shaped the way I saw the world, the way I thought, the way I moved through life.

And even then, I knew one thing for certain: *I wasn't going to follow a blueprint someone else had planned for me.*

CHANGES

3 THE TURNING POINT

'Meditation is our spiritual cleaning agent.'

DEEPAK CHOPRA

As romantic as the beginnings of my life might sound, they alone would not have taken me to where I am today.

My childhood was filled with twists and turns, each more complex than the last, leaving me searching for peace.

My mother's death when I was seven—a final blow after seven years of her battling cancer—shattered the sense of stability I had so desperately clung to. I refused to accept religious comfort or the explanations others offered.

Instead, I became fiercely reliant on instinct.

But life has a way of piling on distractions—material excess, indulgence, and privileges. It felt like sugar, sweet but empty, contaminating the essence of who I was meant to be. I began to see that many of us are lost in life, blinded by what's unnecessary, disconnected from our deeper purpose—our dharma.

And then, one moment changed everything.

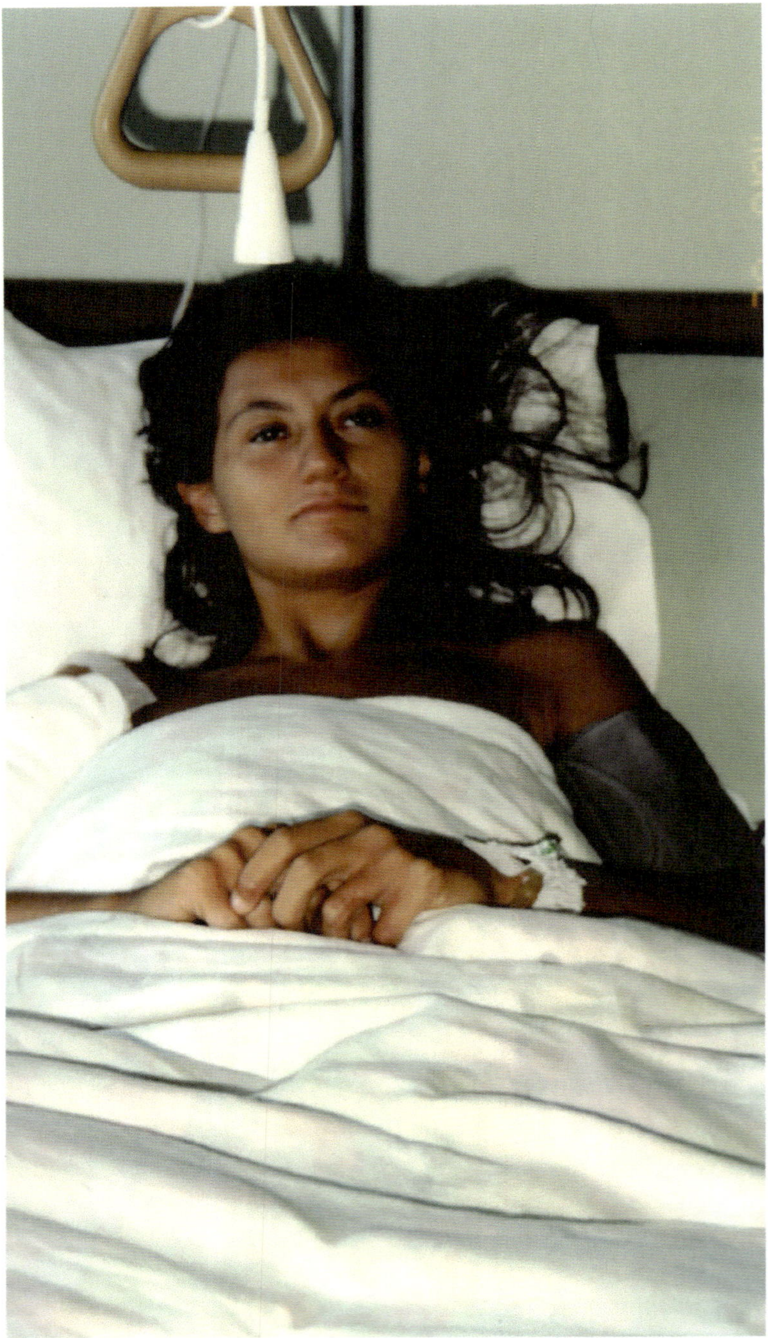

I don't remember the day of the accident.

I've been told it was a wet night, but I don't know where we went, why we went, or how we went. What I do remember is the sensation of falling. It was like being trapped in a dream, plummeting endlessly through darkness at an unbearable speed. It wasn't just physical—it was emotional and spiritual. The pain was too much to feel. My body's instinct for survival took over, wiping out my memories of indulgence, family dramas, academic struggles, and even my sense of self.

All that remained was survival.

When I woke up, I was lying in a hospital bed.

My body felt foreign, and my mind was clouded with confusion. I could recognize three faces: my sister, my brother, and my dad. I knew their faces, but I didn't know who they were. It was as if I was looking at them through a fog. My thoughts were disjointed, and a single feeling echoed in my chest: *Oh my God, not this again.*

I felt suspended between two worlds—the one I had just come back from, a place of light, peace, and weightlessness, and the one I was being dragged back into, a reality of darkness and pain. I didn't belong to this life anymore. I didn't want to. The tension between letting go and being pulled back was agonizing.

Physically, I was tied to the hospital bed.

Left: Recovering after surgery
where all the metal plates were removed
at once at Lindenhof Hosptial.

Emotionally, I began to surrender. My beloved sister, Manuela, acted as my anchor, cushioning my endless fall. But even as she reassured me, I sensed a persistent and torturous feeling that something was wrong.

"Manu," I asked her, "what happened?"

"You had a car crash," she replied. "You're in the hospital recovering."

"Who was in the car with me?" I asked nervously. I was the one who usually drove my friends around.

"Assia and Monica," she said gently.

"How are they?"

"They're in a hospital in Switzerland. They're fine, don't worry."

Her words were meant to comfort me, but they didn't settle. Deep inside, I wondered: If they're fine, why am I here in Italy? Why am I not in the same hospital as them? But I held onto her words. As long as they're okay, that's all that matters.

"You need to focus on yourself," Manu told me firmly. "You've been through a lot. You have many injuries and have already undergone several surgeries."

As I came to terms with my condition, the extent of my injuries unfolded like a horrifying inventory:

- A traumatic brain injury (TBI)
- A cracked right eye
- The right side of my jaw and cheekbone broken
- My left hand fractured
- My left little finger amputated
- My left femur broken
- My right femur broken
- My right wrist broken
- My right humerus broken

Everything was held in place with steel Infibulum, plates, pins and screws to support the healing of fractured femours and homerus.

I had been in a coma for six days. I was completely dependent—unable to walk, lift a glass to drink, or even see clearly. My body had been pieced back together with countless hours of surgery and an arsenal of metal plates and screws. I had no idea how I would move forward, or even if I could.

The emotional weight was just as heavy. Deep down, I felt I wasn't being told the truth. The world felt hollow, and I couldn't believe I would ever walk again, let alone rebuild my life.

My studies, my future—everything I had known was gone.

I didn't know then that this was a turning point.

In the chaos and disorientation, I was being stripped down to the core of who I was. Everything that didn't matter was gone, leaving me with the essential: instinct, survival, and the faintest crumb of hope.

Months later, when I finally learned the truth about Assia and Monica, it hit me with the force of a second collision.

They hadn't survived. The pain was immense. I was disconnected from life, from them, and I was completely lost.

But through the pain flowing in my blood, I found light. Their memory became my guiding beam. I couldn't afford not to live life to the fullest, not when theirs had been cut short. I felt a strength in my body and spirit that I couldn't even explain—it was surreal.

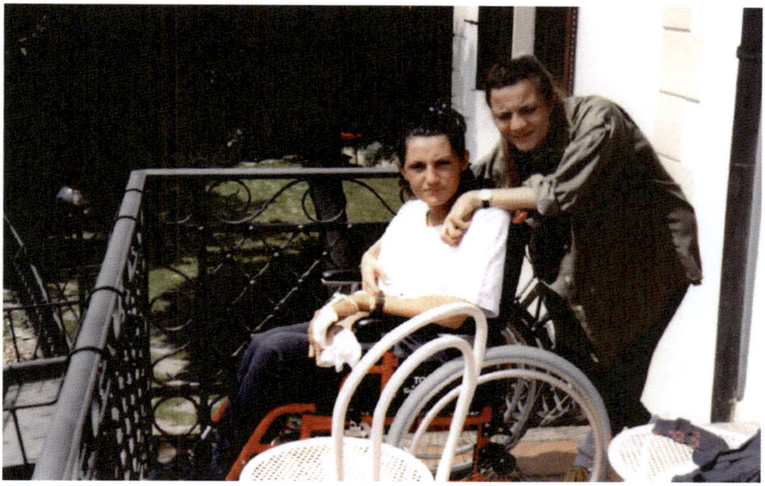

The day my dad told me Assia and Monica hadn't survived.

This experience taught me a profound truth: we aren't in the universe; *we are the universe.* We are focal points where the universe becomes conscious of itself.

That realization was what began to bring me back. I surrendered to the path ahead, trusting that it would lead me to where I needed to be.

THE JOURNEY

4 THE JOURNEY OF HEALING

'Turn your wounds into wisdom.'

OPRAH WINFREY

Recovery is a word that suggests progress, but in reality, it's rarely a straight line.

For me, it was more like navigating a maze—painful, disorienting, and filled with dead ends. I had been told about the extent of my injuries in the hospital, but hearing about them and living through their effects were two very different experiences. The mental confusion, the memory void that I still can't identify to this day—what were we doing?

Where had we been? What happened? Why?

My body felt foreign, as if it no longer belonged to me. Even the simplest of tasks became daunting reminders of my limitations.

Physiotherapy became a daily, unmissable routine, demanding every ounce of my focus and patience. My right arm, locked at a 90-degree angle, had to be stretched and rebuilt over months.

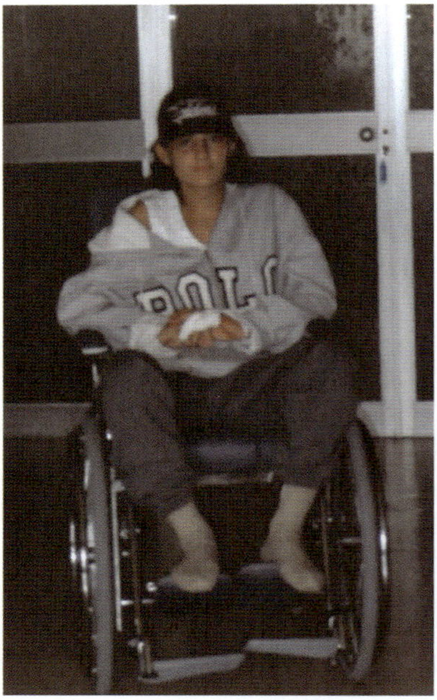

In a wheelchair one month after the accident.

Standing for the first time felt like learning to balance as a one-year-old; I could feel the screws that had been placed through my left knee, especially when I tried to sleep on my side.

That pain taught me to sleep with a cushion between my legs face up—a habit I still follow today, which, as it turns out, is also great for your back.

My scars were never something I was embarrassed about. They were a part of me, a reminder of my strength. But I quickly realized that people saw my scars before they saw me. Their eyes lingered on my legs, my arms, my face—as if my story could only be read through those marks.

But I was so much more than that.

At first, I ignored it. But over time, I noticed how people's expressions changed when they met me for the first time.

Some were curious, some uncomfortable, some even looked away.

Me and Dad.

Even my father, out of love, wanted to protect me from my scars. He arranged for me to see Pitanguy, the most famous plastic surgeon in Brazil, to have them removed. But the moment he suggested it, I said no. He was doing it out of love, but I knew something he didn't.

My scars weren't on me. They were in me.

They weren't something to be erased or hidden—they were part of my story.

It made me realize something important: People are often more uncomfortable with our scars than we are. My scars never made me feel weak—they reminded me I had survived. And yet, the world sometimes looked at them as if they were proof of something broken.

But I refused to let anyone else's perception define me. My scars told a story of resilience, survival, and strength—and I wore them with pride.

(Left) Assia, (Right) Monica and me. My closest friends and my guiding lights. Their friendship shaped me. Their memory continues to inspire me every day.

Emotionally, I was equally lost, but in a different way. The truth about Assia and Monica weighed heavily on me.

When my dad finally told me they hadn't survived, it was a moment of absolute devastation. At the same time, something inside me became startlingly clear: I couldn't go back to my old life. I wouldn't return to studying business. That world, with its focus on profit and structure, no longer made sense to me.

The unanswered questions haunted me, but even if I had found all the answers, it wouldn't have changed the outcome. The lesson was to accept reality for what it was, no matter the unmeasurable collateral damage.

But their deaths left more than grief in their wake—they left guilt. I couldn't shake the pressure of the pain I had caused their families and friends. I felt embarrassed, ashamed, and deeply conflicted about being alive.

I couldn't stop thinking about how many people might have wished it had been me instead of them. The weight of that thought was crushing, and yet I carried it with me, convinced it was part of my penance for surviving.

At the same time, I was in denial. While a part of me was shattered, another part clung to a sense of normalcy.

Less than six months after the accident, I left business school and enrolled in design university, studying Industrial Design. It was a bold move, one that terrified me, but it felt like the first step toward reclaiming my life.

Design became more than a career choice—it became my salvation, the path that ultimately gave me freedom.

Every sketch, every project, every late night spent learning something new was an act of defiance against the darkness that had threatened to consume me. Slowly, I began to see a future I could believe in—a future where I could turn my pain into something meaningful.

For brief periods, I could pretend I wasn't someone recovering from serious trauma. But the falls always came. Occasionally, I would break down, overwhelmed by the reality I was trying so hard to suppress.

It was in these moments that I leaned on my psychiatrist. I saw him once a week for four years, and those sessions became a safety net. They gave me a space to confront the grief and guilt I tried so hard to ignore in my day-to-day life. These conversations helped me understand that healing wasn't about perfection—it was about getting back up after every fall.

In the face of these emotions, I found other tools to help me move forward.

Meditation became crucial for my recovery. I started practicing in 1993, initially to calm my restless mind and help me sleep, but it quickly became much more. Meditation gave me clarity and helped me reconnect with my body, which often felt like a stranger—and, of course, my spirit. It taught me to quiet the noise in my head and focus on the present moment—a skill that became invaluable as I faced the challenges ahead.

Acupuncture was another lifesaver. My first sessions with Dr. Wang were transformative. He taught me exercises to strengthen my back, improve my circulation, and manage my pain. But his message went beyond physical healing. He stressed the importance of 'aging strong', especially for me.

I wasn't just recovering from injuries—I was laying the groundwork for a future where I could thrive, not just survive. His words stayed with me, becoming a mantra as I pushed myself to build a stronger, more resilient body and mind.

These small victories gave me hope that recovery was possible, even if it didn't come easily.

And perhaps the most important tool I discovered was purpose. I realized that I couldn't simply recover for the sake of returning to my old life. I needed to rebuild a new one—one that honoured the two best friends I had lost and the lessons I had learned.

Assia and Monica's memory became my guiding light, their inspiration pushing me to move forward when it felt impossible.

The journey of healing wasn't easy, and it wasn't linear. But with each step, I laid new foundations for my life—stronger and more resilient than before.

Focusing on the feelings in my heart during meditation, in those moments of confusion, ultimately set my future roots.

And as I rebuilt, I carried the memory of Assia and Monica with me, their presence a constant reminder that life, even in its most broken state, is worth living.

Finding strength through stillness – yoga and meditation became essential tools in my journey of healing and self-discovery.

5 CHANNELLING PURPOSE

'You must be the change you wish to see in the world.'
MAHATMA GANDHI

When I left business school, it wasn't just a practical decision to escape pain and memories—it was a declaration, a full dive into the unknown, hoping to find my true direction. I was done living a life built on expectations and obligations, a life that didn't inspire me.

The accident had stripped everything away, and in its aftermath, I was beginning to find clarity—or as I call it now, my spirit level, generated by the alignment of my heart.

If I was going to rebuild, it had to be on my heart's terms.

Enrolling in design university was both terrifying and exhilarating. Before the accident, I had briefly considered studying photography, drawn to the creative freedom it offered. But I had never dared to take the leap.

Now, creativity wasn't just a passion—it was my lifeline.

Design became the thread stitching my life back together.

For most of my life, I never had to think about money.

My father was successful, and I never imagined a future where I would struggle financially. Money was always there, decisions were easy, and I never worried about how things worked.

Until one day, it was all gone.

When my father went bankrupt because of the Asian Financial Crisis 1997, everything changed overnight. Suddenly, I had nothing. No safety net, no backup plan—just myself.

It was a defining moment. I could have stayed in the past, drowning in the loss of what was. But I had a choice: either dwell on what I lost or build something new.

I chose the latter.

I had never worked before, but I quickly realized that hard work and talent weren't enough—I needed to build something that made me irreplaceable. So, I started from zero, piece by piece, determined to create a life on my own terms.

The beginning of my design studies.

REBUILDING THROUGH DESIGN

Starting over meant stepping into an entirely new world. Most of my classmates had been immersed in design for years, while I was beginning from scratch. I didn't have their foundational knowledge, and I often felt like an outsider. But for the first time, I felt deeply connected to what I was doing.

Design gave me something I hadn't felt before: a sense of purpose and enjoyment in what I was doing. It wasn't just about creating beautiful objects; it was about solving problems, about making life better.

That philosophy resonated deeply with me.

But the first projects were humbling.

My hands, still recovering from the accident, didn't always cooperate. Tasks that seemed effortless for my classmates took me twice as long. Yet, I refused to let that stop me. If I couldn't rely on speed or ease, I relied on determination. I poured everything I had into my work, staying late into the night to refine my sketches, make the best of my models, and push myself further.

TURNING EFFORT INTO EXCELLENCE

I wasn't just proving something to myself - I was showing myself what I was truly capable of. Every project became a small victory, a reminder that I could create something new out of the cracks in my life.

My professors noticed. They saw not just the work I produced but the drive behind it. Slowly, I began to gain confidence. I started trusting my instincts, embracing my unique perspective. I wasn't just learning about design—I was finding my voice within it.

One of my proudest moments came with my graduation thesis. After months of relentless work, my design was nominated for the *Compasso d'Oro*, the most prestigious awards in the design world.

The recognition felt surreal.

For the first time, I wasn't just proving something to myself—I was showing the world what I was capable of. It was validation of the effort, the sacrifice, and the belief that I was on the right path.

A CAREER THAT FELT LIKE HOME

What surprised me most was how much I loved it.

For the first time, I was studying something that felt alive. Design wasn't about memorizing facts or following formulas—it was about creativity, intuition, and problem-solving. It was about asking questions and finding innovative ways to answer them—with style.

Designing for the disabled gave me purpose because I could feel the difficulties of moving in space with physical restrictions.

That passion carried me through the toughest moments. When my body ached from long hours at the drafting table or my mind doubted whether I could keep up, I reminded myself why I was here.

I wasn't just studying design—I was building my life.

The accident had taken so much from me, but it had also given me a gift: the opportunity to start over. I had survived, and now I was determined to make that survival meaningful.

Design became my way forward.

As the months passed, I began to see a future I could believe in. Design wasn't just a career—it was a calling.

It gave me a way to channel my pain into something tangible, something that could make a difference.

And for the first time in a long time, I felt hope.

6 FINDING MY FOOTING

'The less you open your heart to others,
the more your heart suffers.'
DEEPAK CHOPRA

When I finally got up from the wheelchair after breaking both my femurs, I noticed something was wrong. My right leg had become three centimetres shorter due to the weight imbalance. I could feel it with every step—I was limping.

I told my father, hoping for reassurance, but instead, he tried to convince me it wasn't true. Maybe he thought it would make me feel better. But I knew my body, and I knew something wasn't right.

The only solution doctors initially gave me? Adding a sole in my shoe.

I knew a simple shoe insert wouldn't fix the deeper problem, and my back was already developing scoliosis. Yet, no doctor seemed able to help—until, through Aram, my brother-in-law, I was introduced to Professor Maurice Müller, the man known as the Orthopaedic Surgeon of the Century.

When he saw me, he didn't hesitate.

He sketched a solution right in front of me, explaining how he could make my femur longer.

Two weeks later, I was at Lindenhof Hospital in Bern, Switzerland, where he performed the surgery.

He broke my femur again and inserted a new metal plate, one that allowed the bone to grow longer naturally.

The surgery didn't just restore my ability to walk—it gave me the confidence to take control of my future. I had faced the impossible and come out stronger. This newfound strength would carry me into my next challenge—building my career.

BUILDING A CAREER IN LONDON

After graduating from design school, I was eager to throw myself into the world of design. I wanted to take everything I had learned—the passion, the creativity, the problem-solving—and see it come to life.

But starting a career is never as glamorous as it sounds.

Milan, though my home and a global design capital, wasn't the right place for me to grow. The system there required years of unpaid work just to get your foot in the industry. I couldn't accept that. My life had taught me the value of time and purpose, and I refused to spend years drawing lines for free. I needed to find a place where my hard work would be recognized and rewarded.

I knew I was going to devote myself, giving no less than 100% of my time, heart, and effort.

In 1997, I moved to London. It was another leap into the unknown, but it felt like the right move. Unlike Milan, where tradition often overshadowed opportunity, London was alive with possibilities.

On a personal level, London gave me the freedom to be myself and explore the taste of life in contrast to the rigid and limiting expectations of my upbringing in Milan. There, tradition and social norms often dictated how one should live, but in London, I found the space to define my own path, embrace diversity, and fully step into who I truly am.

My first job was with a high-end property developer.

I was tasked with designing homes that not only looked beautiful but maximized their value.

Every square meter had to work, not just for the residents, but for the bottom line. It was a crash course in the realities of the design industry. I quickly learned how to balance creativity with practicality, how to make spaces functional without compromising on aesthetics. Every design had to be stunning, yet it also had to be reasonably easy and inexpensive to build. Making the right decisions was paramount. I treated every project like it was my own, with full dedication.

What set me apart was my instinct. Even in those early days, I could see beyond trends and focus on what truly mattered.

My ability to maximize space and create interiors with a wow factor didn't go unnoticed.

The homes I designed consistently sold and rented for top prices. Developers trusted me to deliver results, and that trust gave me the confidence to push boundaries and experiment with new ideas.

But after seven years of working for others, I realized I wanted more control over my projects and independence.

In 2004, I made the jump and set up my own business when I turned 30. This decision marked a turning point. Working directly with private clients allowed me to fully embrace my design philosophy. It wasn't just about creating beautiful spaces—it was about creating homes that felt alive, that reflected the personalities and values of the people who lived there.

TAKING FULL CONTROL

The early years of running my own business were challenging, but somehow, I knew that no matter what, my heart was going in the right direction. My heart would be true to me, and anything led by my heart I could trust.

Like a compass when you are driving a boat in the middle of the sea—if you don't hit the target by even one degree, you end up hundreds of miles away from your target destination. Doing everything in alignment with your focus is what keeps you on course and ensures you reach your goal.

I learned how to manage every aspect of a project, from coordinating builders to ensuring budgets stayed on track. I made mistakes, and there were moments of doubt. Some projects faced unexpected delays; others stretched resources to the limit. But with every challenge, I learned. I learned how to communicate better, how to manage expectations, and how to find solutions when things went wrong.

By 2008, I reached another pivotal moment. Tired of dealing with unreliable and disorganized builders who constantly complicated my life, I realized that continuing under those conditions was unsustainable. I had to make a choice:

- Walk away and find a new career
- Take full control and build something better—because deep down, I knew I loved what I did and had a talent for it.

So, practically overnight, I launched my own building company. It was one of the best decisions of my life. For the first time, I had complete oversight of both design and construction, enabling me to execute projects with unmatched precision, quality, and on budget—consistently exceeding my clients' expectations.

Looking back, those years of transition—from working for others to building my own businesses—were where I truly found my footing. They shaped me into the designer, project manager, and building contractor I am today.

They taught me that great design isn't just about creativity—it's about collaboration, resilience, and a deep understanding of the people you're designing for and the teams you employ to bring those designs to life.

The move to London wasn't just a change of location it was the beginning of a new chapter. It was where I learned to turn my passion into a profession, where I discovered my ability to blend functionality with beauty, and where I began to lay the foundations of a career that would define my life.

London, as a metropolis, allowed me to dive into many different cultures.

These experiences also had a great impact on my designs because they truly allowed my creativity to expand and be adventurous.

AN ADVENTURE BEGINS

7 DESIGNING FOR HIGH-PROFILE CLIENTS – LESSONS FROM THE ELITE

'To be Milanese is to have an innate ability to distinguish the useful from the useless. Being from Milan is almost a philosophy, rooted in a culture of efficiency.'
ALESSANDRO MANZONI

Designing a home is always a deeply personal experience, but when the client is a high-profile figure—a celebrity, a business titan, or a household name—the stakes are even higher. These clients live in the public eye, often in a whirlwind of fast-paced demands, security concerns, and media attention. Their homes are not just places to live; they are retreats, statements, and sanctuaries—spaces where they can escape, recharge, and reconnect with their true selves.

Over the years, I have had the privilege of designing for some of the most influential names in motorsports, entertainment, business, and film.

While their styles, tastes, and personalities varied, one thing remained constant: an uncompromising demand for perfection.

Working with these individuals challenged me to refine my approach, heighten my attention to detail, and push the boundaries of design.

BEYOND AESTHETICS: UNDERSTANDING THE CLIENT'S MINDSET

Designing for high-profile clients goes far beyond selecting fabrics, finishes, or furniture. These are people who operate at an elite level, where every decision is measured for impact, efficiency, and emotional resonance. Their homes must reflect who they are while offering them a reprieve from the public persona they present to the world.

I quickly learned that these clients are extremely intuitive about what they want but often don't have the time to articulate it. They look for designers who understand their lifestyle, habits, and unspoken needs without the need for endless back-and-forth discussions. With some clients, the brief is clear from day one, while with others, it's an evolving process of discovery—one that requires both patience and deep observation.

THE ART OF LUXURY WITHOUT COMPROMISE

One of the biggest lessons I learned from working with elite clients is that luxury is not about excess; it's about precision. It's about making sure that every detail is deliberate, functional, and seamlessly integrated. These clients don't just want a beautiful home—they want a high-performance environment that enhances their lives.

I transformed a seven metre by seven metre reception room into a multifunctional space that seamlessly adapts to different needs—an entertainment area, a home office, and a private cinema. With the touch of a button, it transitions effortlessly into a high-end cinema room, delivering both functionality and luxury. This project exemplifies exceptional space optimization, combining the 'wow factor' with beauty and intelligent design.

NAVIGATING HIGH-STAKES EXPECTATIONS

Recently, a client asked me to manufacture a set of sofas based on a basic sketch of mine—a funky, unconventional shape that I had initially included purely for illustration purposes. To my surprise, they insisted on bringing it to life! What started as a conceptual design became a bespoke reality, proving once again that great design often emerges from the most unexpected moments of creativity

Trust me, a sofa is not something a designer is normally asked to create from scratch. It's a piece that's typically selected, customized, or adapted—but rarely designed entirely from the ground up - and like it wasn't enough a bespoke curved shelving unit was designed as an enclosure turning it into a collector's piece.

PRIVACY, DISCRETION, AND TRUST

Perhaps the most critical aspect of designing for high-profile individuals is *trust.*

These clients value *discretion* above all else.

Their homes are their most private spaces, and they must feel 100% confident that their designer understands and respects that. This is why I never disclose details that would compromise their privacy.

That trust is built over time—by delivering exceptional results, listening attentively, and ensuring that the entire design process remains as seamless and stress-free as possible. In many cases, this trust leads to lasting relationships, with clients returning for future projects or recommending me within their inner circles.

THE TAKEAWAY: EXCELLENCE IS A STANDARD, NOT AN OPTION

What I have learned from working with elite clients is that success is built on precision, discipline, and a relentless commitment to excellence. These are the same principles that apply to life and business as much as they do to design.Whether designing for a world-renowned artist, a CEO, or a private individual with a discerning eye for quality, my approach remains the same:

- **Understand their vision** *beyond* words.
- **Create spaces** that are not only beautiful but *transformative*.
- **Manage expectations** with transparency and deliver *beyond* what was imagined.
- **Ensure discretion, respect, and trust** at *every* stage of the process.

At the end of the day, designing for the world's elite is not about extravagance—it's about mastering the fine balance between luxury, function, and individuality.

And that, to me, is the true art of design.

CLIENT TESTIMONIALS

Patrick Head

"We contracted with ALC Ltd for a complete gutting and redesign of a $500m^2$ Kensington apartment. Once the design was approved, we contracted with ANBM Ltd for an eight-month project, which was completed to a high standard, on time, and on budget. We are very pleased with the service provided by both companies."

Suzan and Morris Nachtomi, California

"Annabella designed two of our homes in London and one in San Diego to our complete satisfaction. We found her to be creative both in design and in finding solutions for our needs. Throughout the project's design and execution, she followed strict budget control and completed the projects on schedule. She is a pleasure to work with—considerate, accommodating, and always available to resolve any issues as they arise."

Sanaz Zaimi, Partner, Bank of America

"Annabella's work is simply unique and timeless. She refurbished my flat ten years ago, and I haven't seen the quality of her finish in any other flat in London. I still get compliments on how modern my flat looks today. She has the rare ability to understand her clients' tastes and adapt her design accordingly. She is extremely reliable, not only during the work but also many years later for maintenance or changes. She is a pleasure to work with, and I highly recommend her."

Judy Choo, Celebrity Chef

"Annabella designed and refurbished my apartment in 2008. She did a superb job in delivering a distinct design that suits both my personal and professional life. She designed a state-of-the-art kitchen where I film my TV cooking program, 'Korean Food Made Simple.' The quality of her construction work is great, and it requires very little maintenance. Her interior design style is unique and timeless."

Patrick and Cathleen Crowley
Hollywood Film Producer

"My wife and I recently spent almost a year at one of Annabella's projects, living in the lovely home designed by Annabella Nassetti. I was producing a movie in London, and every night after a long day on the set, I could look forward to returning to one of the nicest homes we've lived in."

Matteo and Iliyana Stefanel, Apis

We have worked with Annabella and her team for over eight years. Her creativity, her style and approach to design attracted us to her to begin with. Working closely highlighted Annabella's uncanny ability to combine beauty with practicality, clean and linear design with warmth fit for a home, and her vision with the client's requirements and constraints.

8 THE POWER OF FOUNDATIONS

Happiness is not something ready-made.
It comes from your own actions."
DALAI LAMA

A HOUSE ON THE BRINK OF COLLAPSE

It happened in South Kensington, London.

I had been commissioned to excavate a basement, adding an entirely new level to a period terraced house. The project was complex, but everything was progressing smoothly—until it wasn't.

One Friday evening, just as I arrived in the Cotswolds for a much-needed break, my phone rang. It was Paddy, my foreman. His voice, usually steady, carried an urgency that made my stomach tighten.

"Annabella, the concrete pit supporting the 7-meter pillar we fitted today is crumbling."

I froze. We had already removed the temporary supports and secured the house to what should have been a reinforced concrete foundation. If that foundation was now failing, it meant one thing: *the house was at risk of collapse.*

I didn't waste a second. By 8am the next morning, I was back on-site with Terry, our structural engineer. The first step was to re-prop the entire house to stabilize it.

Then, we removed the defective concrete and restarted the process from scratch—at immense cost and effort. The problem? Instead of C35 reinforced concrete, the supplier had delivered C4 mass concrete—a material with zero structural integrity.

Had we not caught it in time, the house could have collapsed, pulling down the neighbouring properties along with it.

Then it hit me: this was more than just a construction disaster averted. It was a lesson in life.

THE FOUNDATIONS THAT HOLD US UP

That moment in South Kensington mirrored a deeper truth I had already lived through.

I remembered waking up after my accident—disoriented, ungrounded, as if the foundation of my entire existence had been wiped out overnight.

Just like that house, I had to rebuild myself from the ground up.

A house is only as strong as the foundation it stands on.

A life is only as strong as the values, mindset, and resilience that support it.

If we build without checking the integrity of our foundations—whether in construction, business, or personal growth—we set ourselves up for collapse.

That realization shaped everything that followed.

- First, **destruction**—when life as I knew it was torn apart.
- Then, the **collapse**—when I had to strip away everything that no longer served me.
- Finally, the **rebuilding**—laying down stronger foundations, physically, mentally, emotionally, and professionally.

This mindset became my **guiding principle**—not just in design, but in *every* aspect of my life. When I started my company, I built it on trust, precision, and integrity—so it wouldn't crumble under pressure.

When I went through depression, I reinforced my internal foundation through meditation, holistic healing, and sheer resilience.

LOOKING AHEAD: A FOUNDATION FOR THE FUTURE

Today, everything I do—whether designing homes, leading my team, or tackling new challenges—is about creating strong foundations.

- In architecture, it's about ensuring stability before adding beauty.
- In business, it's about structuring a vision that can withstand pressure.
- In life, it's about developing resilience before reaching for success.

Because in construction, in business, and in life—the deeper and stronger the foundation, the higher you can build.

9 BOLD DECISIONS AND BREAKING POINTS

'You become what you believe.'

OPRAH WINFREY

Leadership isn't something you're handed—it's something you earn.

By 2008, I had built my own design and building company, giving me full control over the projects I was passionate about. But with that control came immense responsibility. Running a building company wasn't just challenging—it was overwhelming.

The demands felt endless: managing builders, staying on budget, keeping clients happy, ensuring quality, and meeting deadlines—it was like juggling a dozen spinning plates. Many builders had a day-to-day mindset, correcting mistakes half-heartedly, and leaving me frustrated.

No matter how hard I pushed, things always seemed on the edge of chaos.

THE BREAKING POINT

I still remember the moment I almost walked away.

It was a high-stakes refurbishment for an important client—one of those nightmare projects where everything that could go wrong, did.

- Delays piled up.
- Costs spiralled out of control.
- A contractor simply vanished mid-project, leaving me to pick up the pieces.

Every *project* is governed by *scope, specification, time* and *money.* Any issue in just one area... impacts the others. It is an art and a constant stress coordinating, juggling - or controlling - those parameters.

And the stress was suffocating.

One day, I sat in my office, staring at a mountain of paperwork, overwhelmed, asking myself:

"Do I really want this? Is this what my life is going to be?"

I wasn't just exhausted—I felt trapped. I had spent years building something from nothing, yet in that moment, I questioned if it was even worth it.

THE TURNING POINT: A BOLD DECISION

Then, something inside me shifted.

I realized that my frustration wasn't with the work—it was with how I was doing it. I had taken on too much *alone*, trying to do everything myself instead of building the right team.

That's when Flavia came into the picture.

BUILDING STABILITY IN CHAOS

Flavia didn't just bring order to the chaos—she brought stability that extended far beyond the office.

She left behind a secure, successful career to support my vision—a decision that showed her unwavering faith in what we could build together.

For the first time in my life, I felt like I had a foundation I could truly rely on.

Her talent for structure and organization became the backbone of my business.

- She streamlined operations.
- She put efficient systems in place.
- She ensured projects ran smoothly.

Where I thrived in creativity, she thrived in precision. And together, we transformed my company into a well-oiled machine.

Over time, our professional partnership evolved into something deeply personal.

Though our paths eventually diverged, we still work together today. Flavia remains as integral to my business now as she was back then, and I'll always be grateful for the stability and support she brought to my life and career.

THE LESSON: LEADERSHIP THROUGH ADAPTATION

Looking back, that breaking point was one of the most important moments of my career. It forced me to step back, reassess, and delegate.

Leadership isn't about doing everything yourself—it's about

- Building strong foundations
- Surrounding yourself with capable people you trust
- Taking the bold decisions that shape your future

I almost walked away that day — but instead, I built something stronger... on solid foundations.

That experience taught me a crucial lesson: what we see in front of us is never the full story. We must look deeper—whether in leadership, business, or even the spaces we live in.

Strength comes from seeing potential where others see obstacles.

This is the very same skill that has defined my career in design and real estate—the ability to look at a space and see what it could become.

10 THE ART OF SEEING POTENTIAL

'Do what you love, and you'll never work a day in your life.'
CONFUCIUS

From the moment I arrived in London, I found myself drawn to a particular skill—assessing the potential of homes. Viewing houses for clients wasn't just about looking at spaces; it was about seeing *beyond* what was there and envisioning what could be.

Clients trust my vision.

They rely on me not just to evaluate a property's aesthetics but to assess its true potential—what could be done, how much it would cost, and whether it was a worthwhile investment.

Over the years, I have developed an instinct for identifying opportunities that others might overlook.

A cramped Victorian terrace with awkward spaces? I see how walls can be moved to create flow. A dated apartment with low ceilings? I know how to introduce light, open spaces, and make it feel luxurious. A neglected building?

I can envision its transformation and calculate the investment needed to bring it to life.

I have also developed an in-depth understanding of planning consents. By consulting with my trusted planning specialists, who have an impeccable track record of success, I can confidently anticipate which planning applications will be approved. In fact, ten times out of ten, we have secured exactly what I promised my clients—allowing them to move forward with their investment plans with absolute certainty.

This ability to see beyond the surface is one of the most satisfying aspects of my work.

THE VISION CLIENTS TRUST

Real estate agents show houses, but I show possibilities. My experience in design, construction, and project management allows me to walk into a home and instantly analyse:

- What can be done structurally to enhance space and functionality
- How much work is required and an accurate estimate of refurbishment costs
- Where the true value lies in terms of investment and future resale potential
- Which planning permissions can be obtained based on expert insights

Clients trust me because I don't just sell them a vision—I give them real, tangible insights into what's possible.

I've guided investors, homeowners, and developers toward properties with the highest potential, helping them avoid costly mistakes and maximize their returns.

THE SATISFACTION OF TRANSFORMATION

One of the most rewarding moments in my work is when a client sees their finished home for the first time. What was once just a concept—a sketch, a mood board a conversation—becomes a real, living space tailored to their needs and desires.

Every project is a journey. The transformation doesn't just happen to the house—it happens to the people who live in it. I see their excitement grow as their vision takes shape, and when they finally step into their new space, I know I have done my job.

MORE THAN A CAREER, A CALLING

Viewing homes, assessing their potential, and bringing visions to life isn't just a job for me—it's a passion. It's the reason clients keep coming back, the reason I never tire of walking into yet another property, ready to see what others cannot.

But seeing potential is just the first step. The real magic happens when a vision is turned into reality.

That's where *design* comes in.

11 DESIGNING SPACES, SHAPING LIVES

'First you make your beliefs,
and then your beliefs make you.'

MARISA PEER

A home is more than just walls, floors, and furniture—it's a reflection of the people who live within it. For me, designing a house has never been just about creating something visually striking. It's about understanding how people interact with their spaces, how they move, rest, connect, and thrive. A well-designed home isn't just seen—it's felt.

When I started working directly with private clients, I realised how much this philosophy resonated with them. It wasn't just about creating beautiful spaces; it was about creating homes that told their stories. My designs began to focus on blending functionality and emotion, weaving practicality into the fabric of the home while also making it a sanctuary for its inhabitants.

LORENZO CORTE

One of my most memorable projects was for Lorenzo Corte, a Partner at Skadden, and his family. Lorenzo and his wife Sonia wanted their home completely restructured—a project that included everything from a basement excavation to a loft conversion and a full reconfiguration of the house.

A sophisticated and functional living space designed for my dear client Lorenzo Corte – where every element reflects balance,beauty, and purpose.

Lorenzo described it best:

'In two words: *ALC delivered*.

The intelligence of the design and workmanship is superb. The project was completed substantially on budget (less than +5%) and ahead of schedule by two months—even with additional work like a roof replacement. Their proactive, hands-on management meant no delays, and every hurdle was addressed seamlessly. What truly set ALC apart was their design process and management.'

Inspecting on-site structural progress –
ensuring every beam and detail aligns with the vision.

This testimonial reflects what I strive for in every project: combining thoughtful design with meticulous planning and management.

The trust Lorenzo placed in Flavia and me allowed us to create a home that not only met but exceeded his family's expectations. Over the years, my clients have trusted me to bring their visions to life, often giving me 'carte blanche' on their projects. This trust has been humbling and inspiring, pushing me to continually refine my craft.

It quickly dawned on me that one of the most rewarding parts of my work is seeing the impact my *designs* have on the *lives* of the people who live in them.

Work in progress –
transforming space through
creative problem-solving
and meticulous execution.

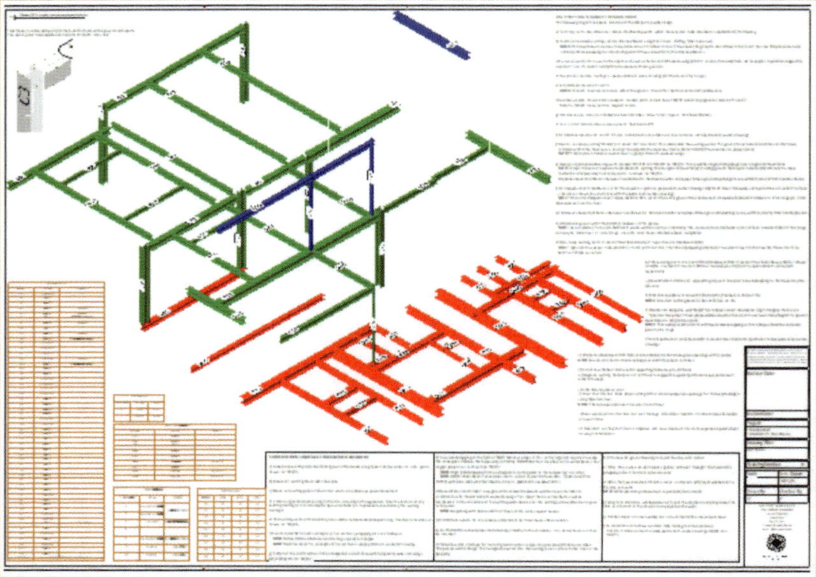

The final transformation – where vision and execution come together to create a harmonious and functional space.

THE ROLE OF ENERGY IN DESIGN

Feng Shui has always fascinated me, but I've come to realise that true harmony isn't just about following traditional formulas—it's about something deeper.

Over the years, I've developed my own understanding of how space and energy interact, one that goes beyond fixed rules and adapts to the individual. I've seen firsthand how the right alignment—both in our environment and within ourselves—can transform the way we feel, perform, and live.

While Feng Shui offers timeless wisdom, I believe there's more to explore—something more personal, more dynamic. And that's exactly what I've been working on.

Looking back, I realise that my design philosophy was shaped by my own journey of healing. The physical challenges I faced after the accident made me deeply attuned to how people move, interact, and find comfort in their environments, or better called in design terms 'ergonomics'—the relationship between us and the objects and space around us. My recovery taught me the importance of balance, structure, and flow—not just in design but in life.

Today, every home I design reflects these values.

I see each project as an opportunity to create harmony, not just in the space itself but in the lives of the people who inhabit it.

Because at the end of the day, a well-designed home isn't just where you live—it's where you truly feel alive.

JUDY CHOO CELEBRITY CHEF

Celebrity Chef Judy Choo in her bespoke kitchen fearturing a five meter steel kitchen... in one piece.

We created a restaurant-style professional kitchen for her London house. The logistics of access and weight were the biggest challenge.

Celebrity chef, Judy Choo had highly specific requirements for a kitchen that had to look good but be fully functional for a professional chef.

A FULLY INTEGRATED APPROACH

We offer a fully integrated *'In-House Design and Build'* service, combining aesthetics with design development using the most advanced 3D software.

Our process includes extensive specifications, architectural and structural packages, and detailed documentation—covering both cost estimation and construction execution. This approach ensures thorough risk assessment, method statements, and full compliance with building regulations and Planning Consent, guaranteeing safety and precision on-site.

What sets our business apart is that we consolidate what typically requires 5-6 separate contracts into a single, seamless agreement. This not only streamlines the process but also eliminates liability issues, legal disputes, costly overruns, and delays—problems that often make projects a nightmare for clients. With us, there are no unexpected extras, just efficiency and peace of mind.

But as I learned, owning property is a different story. You can design the perfect home, ensure every element is in place, and hand over the keys with confidence—but what happens next is out of your control.

And sometimes, what happens next is downright outrageous.

A tenant who thought he could outsmart me, an architect who tried to steal my work, and an unexpected lesson in creative revenge

12 DANCING QUEEN STRIKES BACK

'Buy the ticket, take the ride.'

HUNTER S THOMPSON

Owning and managing property comes with its share of challenges, but nothing could have prepared me for the unexpected drama that unfolded with one tenant. It wasn't just a simple lease violation—it was a personal affront to everything I had built.

It all started when I discovered that my tenant had been subletting my beautifully designed house to an architect. The ultimate insult? This so-called architect was parading the house as his own work.

It wasn't just a breach of the lease—it was a brazen theft of my creativity, my work, and my integrity.

Confronting the tenant directly felt embarrassing and unnecessary. Surely, there was a more creative way to handle the situation—and as it turned out, there was.

One Friday night, after dinner with Flavia at one of

our favourite spots, we decided to walk past the house in question. To our astonishment, we noticed a woman arriving at the front door. Her presence was suspicious, to say the least, and it confirmed what we had suspected: the tenant had turned my home into something entirely inappropriate.

Standing outside my own property, frustration boiling over, inspiration struck. My Control4 app, which allowed me to manage the house's smart systems, came to mind. I pulled out my phone, a mischievous grin spreading across my face, and connected to the house's WIFI.

"What are you doing?" Flavia asked, both curious and concerned.

"You'll see," I replied, trying not to laugh.

Within seconds, I turned off all the lights on all four floors of the house, plunging it into darkness. But I wasn't done yet. I scrolled through the app's music options and found the perfect track for the moment. Moments later, the unmistakable opening beats of ABBA's *Dancing Queen* filled the house at full volume.

From the sidewalk, we watched as chaos erupted inside. The tenant and his 'guest' stumbled around in confusion, likely wondering if the house had been possessed. Flavia and I didn't stick around for long—we left the music blasting and walked away, laughing at the absurdity of it all.

THE AFTERMATH: A SCENE FROM A MOVIE

Three days later, the tenant called to report a 'technical issue' with the house. Reluctantly, I returned to the property, bracing myself for whatever I might find. Nothing, however, could have prepared me for the scene that awaited me.

The house was in complete disarray, as if a wild party had spun out of control. Cocaine residue coated surfaces, oversized adult toys were inexplicably piled in the kitchen sink, and clothes were strewn across every corner of the house.

It was chaos, pure and simple.

I stood there, speechless, and instinctively began taking photos to document the state of the property. It was a surreal moment—a mix of shock, disgust, and an odd sense of vindication.

The tenant eventually moved out, leaving behind nothing but stories that have since become the stuff of legend. To this day, *Dancing Queen* holds a special place in my heart—not just as a classic tune, but as a reminder of the chaos, creativity, and humour that defined one of the strangest moments in my life as a landlord.

Sometimes, life hands you absurd situations, and the best way to handle them is with a sense of humour, a smart app, and a little ABBA.

But as I was about to learn, my misadventures weren't limited to tenants and property disputes. Just when I thought I'd seen it all, life threw me into a real-life heist—this time, the target was my own stolen car.

STEALING BACK THE STOLEN

Some days life hands you an absurd challenge, and all you can do is roll with it. Friday, December 11, 2019, was one of those days.

What began as a normal day ended as one of the most surreal adventures of my life—an impromptu heist to recover my own car.

It all started that morning when I drove to see Rosemary, my spiritual healer. My Mercedes E400, a car I'd come to rely on, was parked outside during the session. When I stepped outside, refreshed and grounded, the car was gone. Stolen.

I stood there in disbelief, Jasper, my loyal Maltese, at my feet. My mind raced. Flavia's face fell when I told her the news. The timing couldn't have been worse. We were days away from leaving for Milan and then the Alps for our Christmas break, with everything meticulously planned: hotels, the journey, and even travel arrangements for our little crew—Jasper and Maui, our cat.

Losing the car threw everything into chaos.

Adding insult to injury, the insurance company informed us there would be no courtesy car for stolen vehicles. Buying a new car on such short notice was out of the question. We were stuck.

A SPARK OF HOPE

That evening, feeling defeated, Flavia and I went to our favourite Spanish restaurant. Over a bottle of wine, the weight of disappointment hung heavy between us. Then, like a flash of inspiration, an idea struck me.

"My Mercedes app sends me notifications when I forget to lock the car," I said, a spark of hope igniting. "Do you think it could tell us where the car is?"

Flavia's eyes widened. I opened the app, my heart racing. And there it was—my car, sitting in North London.

"Abele," I said to the restaurant owner, "keep the wine on ice. We're going to get our car."

THE HEIST

Without a second thought, we hopped into Flavia's tiny Smart car, my spare Mercedes key in hand, and set off. The app guided us to a council estate, a place where shadows loomed large and streetlights barely illuminated the roads.

There it was—my car. The engine was still on, though the lights were off. One window was slightly rolled down. The scene was eerie, like something out of a movie.

Flavia parked the Smart car in reverse, ready for a quick getaway if things went south. My heart raced as I approached the Mercedes. Every instinct screamed at me to turn back, to leave it alone. But I couldn't. The car was locked, and my spare key didn't work. Panic rose in my chest until I remembered the app.

"Please work," I whispered as I opened it.

The app prompted me for a face security scan. With trembling hands, I followed the instructions. Moments later, the app unlocked the car.

I jumped in, adrenaline pumping, and started the engine. Flavia followed close behind, and together we sped away, leaving the scene as quickly as we could.

A TOAST TO THE UNBELIEVABLE

We returned to the restaurant, grinning from ear to ear.

"Abele," I said, handing him the car keys, "you won't believe what just happened."

We finished our bottle of wine, laughing at the absurdity of the night.

The car became our trusty steed for the trip to Milan, pets and all. And in the end, the ordeal became a reminder of one simple truth:

Life is unpredictable, but it's meant to be lived. Sometimes, that means staring fear in the face and taking bold action—even if it's to steal back what's yours.

That night, as I sat in the restaurant, laughing over wine, I realized something: the boldest moves often come when you trust your instincts and take decisive action. It wasn't just about recovering my car—it was about reclaiming control in a moment of chaos. And that's what leadership is, in its purest form. Whether in business, design, or life, leadership is about making bold decisions, trusting your gut, and stepping forward—even when uncertainty looms.

That same philosophy has shaped my journey, not just in my career but on a global scale. Leadership isn't just about managing projects or teams—it's about inspiring change, breaking barriers, and building a future that empowers others. And sometimes, an unexpected opportunity lands in your lap—just as it did when Dr. Harbeen Arora reached out, inviting me to take on a role that would redefine my impact on the world.

13 LEADERSHIP IN DESIGN AND BEYOND

'The feeling that cannot find its expression in tears will cause other organs to weep.'

MARISA PEER

Leadership isn't just about guiding a team—it's about embodying values that inspire others to rise to their full potential.

Over the years, I've realised that my role extends far beyond designing homes or managing construction projects. It's about shaping lives, influencing the next generation, and contributing to a more sustainable and equitable future.

G100 GLOBAL CHAIR

One of the most transformative moments of my career came when Dr. Harbeen Arora, a visionary leader and advocate for gender equality, selected me on LinkedIn to become the *Global Chair* of the *G100 Mission Million – Design and Lifestyle Wing.*

G100

G100—G for *Global* and 100 for *100 industries*—is an international platform dedicated to empowering women across the globe. G100—G for Global and 100 for 100 industries—is an international platform dedicated to empowering women across the globe.

Most Innovative Designer 2021-2022,2022-2023,2024-2025 from LiveWire

Its Mission 'Million Project' seeks to create opportunities, advocate for gender equality, and break down barriers in traditionally male-dominated fields. Being entrusted with this role was a profound honour and a responsibility I embraced wholeheartedly.

For three consecutive years, 2022-2025, I received global awards for *'Most Innovative Designer'*, an acknowledgment of not just my work but the philosophy that drives it. These awards, given by an international community of leaders and visionaries, were deeply humbling.
They validate everything I stand for: *balance, functionality, beauty, and*, most importantly, *purpose* – in the product and the process.

The Mission 'Million Project' create opportunities, advocates for gender equality, and breaks down barriers in traditionally male-dominated fields. Being entrusted with this role was a profound honour and a responsibility I embraced wholeheartedly.

'G100 is a global solidarity for gender equality. Because we don't have to wait 100 years.'

DR HARBEEN AURORA

As Global Chair, I've had the opportunity to lead impactful projects that go beyond traditional design. One of my recent projects, *Enlighten and Reflect*, is a pendant light fitting that embodies the principles of balance and beauty while using sustainable materials.

This project reflects my belief that even the smallest design elements can carry meaning and purpose.

This project was won by a Spanish designer put forward by the Spanish Country Chair of our wing, Contemporary Art Gallerist Mercedes Estarellas.

ASSIAX: FULFILLING MY G100 MANDATE

As the Global Chair of G100 Design & Lifestyle, I founded AssiaX to fulfil the mandate of supporting young talents and promoting sustainability in design.

AssiaX serves as a platform to drive impactful initiatives that align with the G100 mission, fostering innovation and responsible design for a better future.

In a deep conversation with Happiness and Leadership Guru Avinash Ananda. Speaking at the White Page International leadership conclave- a platform to share my journey and inspire others through design, resilience and innovation.

Receiving a leadership award in Dubai – and global recognition for contribution to design, sustainability, and leadership.

Presenting *Enlighten & Reflect* my G100 project developed through AssiaX. The sustainable light fixture embodies balance, beauty, and purpose, aligning with my wisdom for impactful design

London Light for Life for AssiaX is a pilot project aimed at redesigning London's lamp posts to bring biodiversity into the city. These multifunctional, part-solar-powered lamp posts are designed to create bee lines by incorporating greenery and habitats for pollinators.

London is serving as the testing ground for this innovative idea, but our vision is to export it to other cities around the world. It's a project that combines sustainability, functionality, and ecological restoration—a true reflection of how design can contribute to a healthier planet.

Angus Cunningham from Scotscape is currently in the process of producing the lamp-posts in London.

This project was awarded to a young Swiss designer who was put forward by the Swiss Country Chair of our wing, an artist with great talent, Serena Maisto.

I am very proud to be working with and for dear sister Dr. Harbeen Arora, Founder, G100 | Women Economic Forum knowing that this is what she thinks of me:

"Annabella Nassetti is a visionary leader whose work in design extends far beyond aesthetics. Spiritually centred and connected to community, she is an ardent supporter and mentor for young women in design, enabling them to find new opportunities through innovation and self-belief. Her book, *Foundations of Life*, is an expression of the meaningful change she seeks - not just in spaces, but in people's lives."

Dr. Arora's vision and leadership have deeply inspired me. Her ability to bring together leaders from across 100 industries to advocate for women globally is nothing short of extraordinary.

She believed in me and gave me the platform to amplify my voice and values on an international stage.

What I've learned through my leadership journey is that design, at its core, is about problem-solving. Whether I'm creating a home, mentoring a young professional, or collaborating on a global initiative, my goal is the same: to bring clarity, balance, and purpose to the chaos.

Take, for instance, the project that earned me my first leadership award in Dubai.

During my acceptance speech, I shared how a devastating accident had reshaped my life and how I turned that pain into purpose.

Standing on stage with Happiness and Leadership Guru Avinash Ananda, I wasn't just representing myself—I was representing the values that have guided me through every challenge: resilience, creativity, and the courage to start over.

These moments of recognition remind me of how far I've come, but they also remind me of the responsibility I carry. Leadership is about more than achievements; it's about paving the way for others. It's about turning your experiences into lessons and your success into opportunities for others.

One of the most fulfilling aspects of my work has been the chance to mentor young women entering the design and construction industries. As someone who navigated these male-dominated fields with little guidance, I know how crucial it is to have a role model, someone who believes in you and encourages you to take up space.

My leadership philosophy is simple:

Lead with purpose, listen with intention, and act with integrity.

Whether I'm designing a home, managing a team, or delivering a keynote speech, these principles guide me.

Looking ahead, I see my role not just as a designer, project manager, and builder, but as a leader committed to creating a ripple effect of change.

Through my work with G100 Mission Million - Design and Lifestyle Wing, my advocacy for sustainability, and my dedication to mentoring the next generation, I hope to leave a legacy that extends far beyond the walls of the homes I've built.

Because at the end of the day, leadership isn't about titles or accolades—it's about impact. It's about the lives you touch, the values you uphold, and the change you inspire. And that, more than anything, is what keeps me moving forward.

BEYOND LEADERSHIP: A DEEPER TRANSFORMATION

While my work in design and leadership had created real impact, something inside me was shifting.

The more I empowered others, the more I realized that transformation wasn't just about buildings, projects, or leadership roles—it was about people.

It was about healing.

I had spent decades designing spaces for harmony, but I hadn't yet fully addressed the *internal* architecture of my own life.

This realization became impossible to ignore when my past caught up with me—forcing me to confront emotional wounds I had long buried.

What happened next reshaped everything: my perspective, my purpose, and ultimately, my career.

It wasn't just about building homes anymore—it was about rebuilding myself.

THE NEW VISION

14 EXPANDING THE VISION

'Have the courage to follow your heart and intuition. They somehow already know what you truly want to become.'

MARISA PEER

Looking back on my journey, I see that every challenge, every breakthrough, and every decision has led me to where I am today.

My work has always been about more than just designing homes or managing construction projects—it's about creating a legacy of purpose, inspiration, and impact.

For 25 years, I lived in 'coping mode', shielding myself from the pain of my past.

Surviving a life-altering accident pushed me into a state of emotional detachment. It allowed me to build a career and a life, but it also kept me from fully feeling. When those walls finally cracked, the flood of emotions—grief, fear, and pain—was overwhelming. It was a deep reckoning, but it was also the beginning of true healing.

That period of depression forced me to pause.

The coping mechanisms that had sustained me no longer worked.

I had to find a new way forward, one that wasn't just about survival but about truly living. Meditation, time in nature with my Maltese Jasper, and holistic practices like Rapid Transformational Therapy (RTT) became my lifeline.

RTT was a game-changer—it helped me break through limiting beliefs and reconnect with my true self. I discovered the power of our thoughts and as simple as it sounds, it works. Like a flash of clarity, it revealed exactly what I wanted.

'When you control your thoughts, it changes your whole life. When you make your thoughts positive you make your life extraordinary.'

MARISA PEER

THE POWER OF HEALING: ACUPUNCTURE AND SCARS

Healing isn't just about moving forward—it's about releasing blockages that prevent us from thriving.

Just as a building's foundation must be cleared of weaknesses before construction begins, our bodies and minds require deep recalibration to function at their best.

I discovered acupuncture many years ago, and it has been a cornerstone of my well-being by restoring Inner Harmony within me. It offers a powerful way to reignite balance and vitality by targeting the body's energy pathways.

Daily habits and stress can create blockages that disrupt the natural flow of blood and energy, leading to tension and imbalance.

By skilfully piercing specific points where blockages occur, acupuncture releases trapped heat and reduces inflammation, allowing the body to heal and restore its optimal flow. This ancient practice clears the pathways of both mind and body, promoting harmony, clarity, and vibrant well-being.

Like RTT, acupuncture treats the root cause, not the symptom, which is the only way to permanently address the presenting problem, drug-free.

Unlike many health conditions treated with pharmaceuticals, which often address the symptom while inadvertently harming other organs. Scars—whether physical or emotional—hold memories of trauma. They can be protective, but they can also trap energy, keeping us in patterns of pain and limitation.

Rapid Transformational Therapy (RTT), much like acupuncture, works by accessing the root cause of these scars, releasing the trapped energy, and allowing true healing to take place.

Just as I have designed homes for balance and flow, I now help people redesign their inner world for clarity and renewal.

This transformation wasn't just personal; it reshaped my professional outlook. I realised that my work wasn't just about creating beautiful spaces—*it was about balance and harmony, both in design and in life.*

That realisation led me to expand my vision beyond design and construction, embracing coaching as a natural extension of my work.

Coaching, like design, is about transformation.

It's about guiding people to break through limitations, to see possibilities where they once saw obstacles. Just as I design homes to be functional and inspiring, I now help people design lives that align with their purpose. This shift felt natural because the principles are the same: strong foundations, clarity, and intentionality.

Sustainability has also become a key pillar of my work. Projects like *London Light for Life* and *Enlighten and Reflect* prove that even small design choices can have a lasting impact. My goal is to create not just for today, but for the future—to leave a meaningful footprint that extends beyond aesthetics.

As I continue to build, coach, and design, my purpose is clear: to inspire others to see that no matter how broken things may seem, they can always be rebuilt—stronger, better, and with deeper meaning. Because in the end, it's not just about what we create, but about the foundations we leave behind.

More recently, just when I thought I had figured it all out, I found myself questioning everything I believed in.

I had no idea that such deeply toxic personality traits could exist, and I was jolted into a surreal reality—one shaped by the grip of a narcissistic relationship. I doubted everything about myself, and I had never felt so deeply hurt. Yet, deep inside, I knew it wasn't me—the situation was so surreal that I could hardly believe it was happening. I felt stupid, trapped in a reality that didn't make sense. And until my physical safety was at risk, I couldn't bring myself to make the move and detach.

But the moment I was put in danger, something shifted.

My heart and mind aligned instantly, and I walked away without hesitation. I was still hurting, but I was no longer lost. No second-guessing. No hesitation. Just clarity.

Narcissism isn't something you can fix in someone. It's a disorder.

That's when I realized something crucial: narcissistic traits should be taught to be identified because they can be truly harmful and young people should be made aware of the characteristics:

- **Gaslighting** (Distorting Reality)
- **Lack of Empathy** (Emotional Coldness)
- **Love-Bombing & Devaluation** (The Cycle of Control)

If you experience anything along those lines, one word of advice:

Recognize. Tag. Run.

Because if you don't, you risk losing yourself before you even realize what's happening.

FROM SURVIVAL TO SELF-MASTERY

Walking away from that relationship wasn't just about escaping toxicity—it was about reclaiming myself. It forced me to confront the deeper question: How had I, someone so strong, ended up doubting my own reality?

The answer lay in my past, in the subconscious patterns I had unknowingly carried for years.

But this wasn't just about looking back.

It was about moving forward with clarity, confidence, and the understanding that true power isn't about control—it's about self-mastery.

It was time to rewrite the script.

15 NOURISHMENT BEYOND THE PLATE

'You can't connect the dots looking forward; you can only connect them looking backward.'

STEVE JOBS

A NOTE OF GRATITUDE

There's one more piece of my journey I feel compelled to share—something that has quietly supported every transformation I've made: nutrition.

This chapter is written in part with the influence of Flavia, someone who introduced me to the world of organic food. I want to give her full credit for planting this seed in me. She is an extraordinary creative and instinctive cook. Her passion about ingredients—inspired a deeper awareness in me about what nourishment really means.

Flavia worked for Lady Carole Bamford, a entrepreneur and philanthropist renowned for her contributions to sustainable living and organic farming.

Daylesford Organic Farm & Bamford, a place known not only for its organic philosophy but for its exceptional attention to detail, sustainability, and aesthetics. Flavia's time at Bamford left a strong impression.

There was something deeply aligned with my own sensibilities in the lifestyle, the beauty of the interiors, the care in the food, and the way everything came from a place of integrity and elegance.

NOURISHMENT AS A FOUNDATION

Long before I stepped fully into fitness or healing, I was already becoming more conscious of what I was putting in my body. It started almost instinctively—as I moved away from processed, packaged foods and became more curious about ingredients, labels, and the origin of what I was eating.

The idea of food being grown naturally, without synthetic chemicals, resonated with me. It felt right—not just for my health, but for the Earth. I found myself drawn to organic produce, local ingredients, and whole foods in their most natural form. Even before I understood the science, I could feel the difference: better energy, digestion, skin, and mood.

As I deepened my fitness journey, it all began to connect. I realized that strength, performance, recovery, and mental clarity were built not just in the gym, but on the plate. I started learning more about macronutrients—proteins, carbs, and fats—and how to balance them. I became aware of micronutrients too: the essential vitamins and minerals that support everything from hormone regulation to immune strength.

My approach to food became less about perfection and more about intention. It wasn't about fads or restriction—it was about fuel. It was about self-respect. It was about choosing what made me feel truly good.

And it showed. My energy stabilized. My sleep improved. My workouts felt stronger, more effective. But even more than that—my mind felt calmer. My mood lifted. My sense of alignment deepened.

A CONSCIOUS CHOICE

Choosing organic and local isn't just a personal benefit—it's a conscious decision to support sustainable farming and ethical food systems.

When we nourish ourselves well, we're also nourishing the planet.

That's why I say nourishment goes far beyond calories or macros. It's about wholeness. It's about balance. It's about reconnecting with your body and the Earth that sustains it.

So, if you're on a journey toward wellness or reinvention, don't overlook your plate. It's not just about aesthetics—it's about energy, clarity, and resilience.

Start small. Stay curious. Listen to your body. And always remember: *what you put in, you get out.*

With gratitude to Flavia, to the teachers and experiences that shaped this part of my path, and to food itself—for being one of the most beautiful, powerful tools for transformation.

Stay tuned—this chapter is only the beginning. We will be integrating these principles into a new wellbeing and lifestyle program, designed to help you align your life from the inside out.

16 CLOSING THE CIRCLE FROM TALENT TO PURPOSE

THE THREE PHASES OF GROWTH

Looking back, I can see my life unfolding in three distinct phases — each one leading naturally into the next. It wasn't always obvious at the time, but now, as I step fully into my purpose, I realise that everything I've done has been building toward this moment. The circle is closing. The journey is coming full circle, all because of authentic growth and acceptance of life.

1 TALENT – THE GIFT OF DESIGN

From a young age, I was drawn to beauty, space, and structure. Design wasn't just something I studied—it was a natural instinct, an extension of who I was. My gift led me to study design, and my accident gave me the clarity to pursue it without hesitation.

2 CAREER – DETERMINATION & FOUNDATIONS

Talent alone isn't enough.

Success requires determination, resilience, and a strong foundation.

Moving to London, building my career, and later launching my own design and build company was about more than just creating beautiful spaces. It was about taking control, solving problems, and proving that I could succeed in an industry dominated by men. It was about understanding structure—not just in buildings, but in business and in life.

The lesson I learned? A strong foundation is essential for everything—whether it's a home, a career, or a life. I applied the same principles of architecture to my own journey: stability, precision, and purpose.

But after years of pushing forward, I found myself searching for something deeper. I had built a successful career. Yet, something was missing.

3 PURPOSE – COACHING AND RTT

For years, I thought that my work was about designing houses. Then I realised I was designing lives.

Everything changed significantly when I discovered Rapid Transformational Therapy (RTT). After years of psychology and traditional therapy that never seemed to go deep enough, RTT unlocked something in me instantly. It was like removing a block that had been holding me back... *for years.*

RTT, combined with my long-standing practice of meditation, energy work, and holistic healing, showed me that transformation isn't just about the external world—it starts within.

(Left)With World-renowned therapist, best-selling author, and Founder of Rapid Transformational Therapy (RTT), Marisa Peer, Rushton 2024.

Now, I see my work differently.

Whether I'm designing a home, working with a client in RTT, or guiding someone toward change, the goal is always the same: to create balance, clarity, and transformation.

This is why my approach is unique.

I don't just design homes.

I don't just coach people.

I design lives.

17 CONCLUSION: THE FOUNDATIONS OF LIFE

We have one life, and we are in the driver's seat.

Every decision, every step forward, is ours to make.

We may not control everything that happens to us, but we always control how we respond. And in those responses—in the choice to rise, to rebuild, to create—we shape our lives and leave our legacy.

At the heart of this journey is a simple truth: for every right we enjoy, there's a responsibility we must embrace. But responsibility isn't a burden—it's what gives life purpose.

Achievement isn't about shortcuts or luck; it's about commitment, resilience, and taking ownership of our choices.

Life isn't just about what we receive—it's about the value we add.

The Power of Inner Strength Power is not something external—it is generated from within. True transformation comes from harnessing that inner power, from aligning our thoughts, energy, and actions with clarity and purpose. Force is imposed. Power is intrinsic.

When we tap into that power, we stop chasing success and become the source of it. I've tested this in my own life. I've lived it. And I can confidently say—it works.

Designing Your Life Every foundation you lay, every decision you make, every challenge you overcome—it all prepares you for what's to come.

The journey itself is what gives life meaning.

- Your life is your masterpiece
- Build it with intention
- Design it with love
- Live it with courage
- And never stop evolving

As I continue this journey, I am now integrating Meta Mind into my Self-Leadership and Energy Coaching Program alongside RTT, bringing a deeper level of self-mastery and transformation.

This is not just a coaching experience—it's a complete recalibration of how we lead our lives.

At the core of true transformation lies self-leadership—the ability to align mind, energy, and actions with clarity and purpose.

My program combines:

- **Energy Alignment** – Body and mind to harmonize internal balance.
- **Rapid Transformational Therapy (RTT)** – to reprogram subconscious beliefs.
- **Meta Mind** – the MIND framework, created by Avinash Ananda, to master personal and professional success.

This program isn't for those looking for quick fixes. It's for those ready to take full ownership of their lives.

NO SHORTCUTS IN LIFE

If you believe shortcuts exist, you've already set yourself up to fail. Success is built through dedication, resilience, and deep inner work. The journey matters just as much as the destination—because if you don't walk the path, you won't be ready to receive what's at the end.

As this book comes to a close, my next chapter is just beginning.

- The foundation is solid
- The design is in plac.
- And now, it's time to live in full alignment—with talent, career, and purpose as one

OWNING YOUR UNIQUE POWER

Every single one of us has unique traits, talents, and gifts. But the real magic happens when we stop trying to fit into Molds that aren't ours and start shaping our own identities.

For years, I focused on building my skills—design, business, leadership. But what set me apart wasn't just my experience. It was how I saw the world, how I connected dots others couldn't see, how I instinctively knew what worked.

Success isn't about being the best at everything. It's about owning what makes you extraordinary.

But here's the secret: You can only discover your gifts by connecting with your inner being.

Every day, I take time to go inward—to sit with my thoughts, to listen to what my body and intuition are telling me.

This practice has guided me more than any business strategy ever could.

Daily meditation is the key—it aligns your energy, clears the mental noise, and helps you tap into the true source of your strength. I built my career by embracing what made me different, by refining my instincts and transforming them into a signature approach.

That's how I created my brand. If there's one thing I want people to take away, it's this: *Make the best of your gifts.*

- Tap into your strengths
- Build your own identity. Because when you tune in instead of looking outward for answers, you create something no one else can]

The circle has closed.

And a new one begins.

18 THREE TURNING POINTS

Every life has defining moments. Mine came in three waves.

- **The Accident – age 19.** The moment that took the ground from beneath my feet—literally and metaphorically. It marked the start of my *coping mode*, a protective numbness that carried me through years of survival.
- **My father's Bankruptcy – age 25.** This stripped me of security and taught me how to rebuild from nothing. It was the moment I chose independence over fear.
- **The Awakening, the end of Coping Mode** – age 45. After 25 years, I *felt* again.

The pain I had buried came rushing back, and it was through this pain that I finally began to heal. This was the moment I chose to live, fully and freely.

These three turning points shaped the woman I am today.

The conclusion? Annabella's ability to turn pain into purpose and adversity into growth is captured beautifully in her latest pitch—her life, her mission, and her message.

WHAT MADE ME AND WHAT I'M HERE TO DO.

Everything I've lived — shaped who I am.

But none of it defines me. What defines me is what I did with it.

I didn't change my career. I transformed how I show up in it. I am still a designer. I am still a builder. But I am also something more.

I now bring together architecture, project management, emotional intelligence, and energetic alignment.

I don't just build homes—I create spaces that support wholeness. I don't just coach—I help people create lives that support their truth.

This isn't a pivot. It's a natural evolution.

I've integrated what I've learned from pain, healing, success, trauma, and deep inner work—and turned it into a complete approach to helping people thrive, both in their space and in their self.

At the core of everything I offer—whether it's a luxury design-build project or a transformational coaching session—are the values that saved and shaped me:

- **The Truth in Objectivity** – the clarity to see things for what they are.
- **Take Ownership and Accountability for my Decisions.**
- **Omni-love** – the unconditional love I now extend to others, because I finally gave it to myself.

These three pillars are not just values.

This is the MetaMind Method and a method I recognise has been in me and played a crucial part in my holistic recovery.

This is how I help people move from misalignment to clarity, from clutter to flow, from surviving to living fully.

So if you're here at the end of this book wondering how my story connects to yours...

The answer is simple: I'm not special. I'm just awake. And if I did it—you can too.

Let's build something extraordinary—together.

From the inside out.

19 ROSEMARY, HEALING AND CONNECTION

Me and Rosemary Warcup.

Some of the most powerful healing doesn't happen in solitude—it happens in presence.

In holding space for someone else. In showing up with love, when words are no longer enough.

One of those sacred moments came in the final days of a beloved friend. I stood beside Rosemary, the woman who had first introduced me to energy healing and intuitive alignment—this time, not as a seeker, but as a giver.

Together, alongside Natalie Imbruglia, Caroline, Iren, Bawo, and many others, we held space for Rosemary during a month where love and grief coexisted in their rawest form.

What we experienced was beyond technique. It was presence. It was energy. A profound, unspoken connection that brought light even into the most painful goodbye.

During those four weeks, something in me opened. I wasn't just witnessing my spiritual healer's final days—I was living her pain alongside her. I would have done anything to fulfil her last wishes: to bring her home, to give her the peace she so deeply deserved, and to support her in letting go of life with dignity and love.

My heart expanded as I saw how many lives she had touched—thousands. The ripple of her work, her soul, her generosity.

When the time came to organise her funeral, I made sure that the people she had helped knew. She hadn't told anyone she was unwell. She hadn't wanted pity—only presence.

Coordinating her final farewell was one of the most painful and important acts of love I've ever carried out. And what formed in that shared sacred space—between her friends, her healers, her soul family—was something intangible but unbreakable. A bond made eternal through love and service.

It became a lifelong reminder of the beauty that lives in vulnerability, compassion, and connection.

It remains one of the most difficult, and most meaningful, experiences of my life.

20 EPILOGUE

We've reached the end of this memoir—but truly, this is just the beginning.

As with everything I do, I only step in when I can offer a real solution. Whether it's in design, construction, or a life that feels out of alignment, I've always had the ability to see through complexity and bring clarity—serving friends, family, and anyone who's ready for change.

I now stand not only as a designer, but as a guide. A woman who rebuilt herself—physically, mentally, emotionally—and now helps others do the same. My path to fulfillment was built on instinct, determination, and the unwavering choice to follow my heart.

As human beings, we are among the most intricate creations in existence. When in balance, our systems perform with grace and ease. The mind and body are deeply connected—like an instrument that, when attuned, produces resonance. I've come to learn that there are ways to calibrate this connection, creating a personalized formula for balance and lasting fulfilment.

I speak from experience—because I've lived this transformation.

It's easy to think we must control every part of life, but in truth, surrender often leads us exactly where we're meant to go. As The Rolling Stones so perfectly put it:

'You can't always get ..."

Life may not unfold as we planned—but it always delivers what we're ready for.

And now, more than ever, we have the tools to meet it fully.

- Rapid Transformational Therapy
- Coaching
- Meditation
- Movement
- Nutrition

These aren't just practices—they're pathways. They help us reclaim peace, vitality, and purpose—without dependency on medication, but through daily rituals that keep us strong and aligned.

When we reconnect with our bodies and clear the noise of our minds, something beautiful happens: life flows. With the right tools and guidance, you can live your truth, your rhythm, your deepest joy.

This is what I want for you. Take what you've read in these pages and begin.

Begin building the life you're meant to live—with clarity, confidence, and heart. If you're ready, I'm here. Let's take the next step together.

NEXT STEPS

CLARITY, CONFIDENCE, AND ALIGNMENT MY INVITATION

I'm Annabella Nassetti—award-winning Product Designer, Interior Architect, certified RTT Therapist, Self-Leadership Coach, and Author. For over 25 years, I've helped exceptional clients transform not only their homes, but often, their lives.

My work is rooted in a simple truth: alignment matters.

In our homes. In our mindset. In our energy. In our choices.

FROM DESIGN TO TRANSFORMATION

I built my career through a unique 360° turnkey model—seamlessly integrating design, project management, and construction under one roof. One contract. One point of contact. One aligned vision. This approach eliminates the chaos, stress, and fragmentation that so often derail high-end renovation projects.

But my journey didn't stop with beautiful interiors.

A life-altering accident in my early twenties reshaped the way I viewed space—not just as physical, but emotional, energetic, and deeply personal. That awakening led me to explore Rapid Transformational Therapy, energy alignment, and self-leadership.

Today, I offer something rare: a way to align both your inner world and outer environment—so they work together in harmony.

WHY IT MATTERS

Most renovations involve multiple professionals, clashing agendas, missed deadlines, and mounting stress. What should be a joyful transformation becomes overwhelming.

I remove that complexity.

I design not just stunning spaces—but deeply intentional sanctuaries. When your space is aligned, you are aligned. When your mind is clear, your home supports you. When your energy flows, life moves forward.

My clients range from Formula One engineers to international lawyers and high-profile creatives. But most importantly, they are people ready to live more consciously—who want their homes to reflect not just success, but soul.

Many return again and again. That trust is the true measure of my work.

A LIFE REBUILT. A MISSION REDEFINED.

What once felt like devastation became the foundation for everything I've built.

I turned pain into purpose. Loss into legacy. Survival into service.

Now, I help others do the same.

Whether you work with me to transform your home or your life—I meet you where you are, and guide you to where you are meant to be.

LET'S DESIGN YOUR NEXT CHAPTER

If this speaks to you, here's how to begin:

- Send me a photo of your home or space.
- Complete a short, insightful alignment workshop.
- If your score is five or below, we'll schedule a free 45-minute discovery consultation.

Your life is too precious to live in a space—or a state—that no longer supports you.

I'm here to help you realign.

I'm a home and mind doctor.

Let's design your next chapter—from the inside out.

- For design and build projects *www.abnassetti.com*
- For transformational coaching and RTT therapy *www.abnassettithecoach.com*

Both paths are available individually—or combined into one powerful, integrated solution.

WHAT'S NEXT?

As for me, the journey continues.

My next book, *Follow Your Heart*, will go deeper into the power of intuition and emotion. Because if the mind creates our reality, it is the heart that defines how we truly live it.

Are you ready to take the next step?

Let's continue this journey together.

Visit *AbnassettiTheCoach.com* to explore my coaching programs, book a discovery call, or connect with me personally. Whether you seek clarity, healing, or lasting transformation—I am here to support you.

If you ever find yourself at a crossroads, wondering which direction to take, know this:

You are not alone.

When you're ready, we'll walk the next part of your path together.

With all my heart,

Annabella

THE HAPPINESS COMPASS

CHECK YOUR ALIGNMENT

Before you turn the final page, I invite you to pause and gently check in with yourself.

You've walked through my story. You've seen what's possible when we stop coping and start realigning. Now, let's take a moment to look inward — with honesty, without judgment.

The *Happiness Compass* is a simple yet powerful tool to reflect on your current state across six essential dimensions of life. It's not a test. It's a mirror. *The Happiness Compass* (your adapted wording, safe to use)

Rate yourself from 1 to 10 in each area below:

1 = Unfulfilled or out of alignment

10 = Deeply fulfilled and aligned

Area	**Your Score 1-10**
Mind & Emotions (Psychological)	
Purpose & Work (Professional)	
Relationships (Social)	
Body & Vitality (Physical, health, vitality))	
Spiritual Connection (Purpose, growth)	
Financial Flow (Material)	

REFLECT & REALIGN

- What areas feel strong? What feels neglected?
- What's one small action you can take this week to raise one score by just 1 point?
- What would life feel like if all these areas aligned?

IF YOUR AVERAGE SCORE IS 5 OR BELOW...

- This isn't a sign of failure — it's a call for support.
- It means your inner compass is asking to be realigned. And that's exactly what I do.
- If this exercise revealed a gap, I would be honored to help you fill it — with clarity, courage, and joy.
- Book your free 30-minute Clarity Call at *https://abnassetti.com/contact/*

Because life isn't meant to be coped with.

It's meant to be *designed.*

ABOUT ANNABELLA NASSETTI

Born in Milan, Annabella Nassetti grew up immersed in beauty, functionality, and a lifestyle culture that shaped her instinct for design and harmony from an early age.

Initially set on a business career, a profound and life-altering experience led her to shift paths—awakening her passion for creation, transformation, and ultimately, her purpose.

Annabella became a product designer and interior architect, quickly rising to success in the world of high-end architectural interior design and property development in London.

With a unique ability to maximise spatial layouts for both energy flow and market value, she earned a reputation for delivering record-breaking results over two decades. Her deep commitment to excellence, combined with a visionary eye, led her to establish her own in-house construction company in 2008—streamlining every stage of the process from design through to delivery. This hands-on approach built long-standing trust and loyalty with clients who have returned to her time and again for over 20 years.

What sets Annabella apart isn't just her design sensibility, but her knowledge of construction, materials, and energy alignment. She masterfully bridges form and function, style and soul—creating spaces that are not only beautiful, but deeply nourishing.

Annabella is an award-winning interior architect. She was awarded the *Most Innovative Designer* (2022–2025), *Global Power Leader - The House of Lords* (2024 & 2025), *Woman Entrepreneur of the Year - Dubai* (2024), *Global 200 Inspirational Leader - Dubai* (2023), and *Woman of the Decade - London Women Economic Forum* (2023).

And she is currently the Global Chair for *G100 Mission Million Project - Design and Lifestyle Wing* that fosters and mentors and creates opportunities for young professional women.

In recent years, Annabella underwent a powerful personal transformation. Through deep reflection, she embraced a new calling: helping others awaken, realign, and reclaim their power. She became a certified RTT® Therapist and Self-Leadership Coach, merging her design expertise with emotional and energetic mastery into a unique approach she calls *House and Lifestyle Design*.

Today, she is an award-winning Interior Architect *and* an RTT® Therapist, Self-Leadership Coach, and Speaker.

Find Your Heart, Foundations of Life - Building Dreams, Transforming Lives, is a testament to how life's deepest challenges can become the blueprint for our greatest becoming. It is both an intimate account and an inspiring guide for anyone ready to turn pain into purpose and design a life they truly love.

CONTACT ANNABELLA NASSETTI

For design and build projects
www.abnassetti.com
info@ abnassetti.com

For transformational coaching and RTT therapy
www.abnassettithecoach.com

Printed in Great Britain
by Amazon

62935838R00085